MAKESHIFT
Galaxy

For Moomin,
who taught me how to love the stars,
and reach for dreams beyond them.

PUBLISHER
OBSCURA

Published by Publisher Obscura in 2017
An imprint of Odyssey Books

www.publisherobscura.com

National Library of Australia
Cataloguing-in-Publication entry
Author: Turgoose, Tash
Title: Makeshift Galaxy / Tash Turgoose
ISBN: 978-1-925652-15-4 (hardcover)

MAKESHIFT *Galaxy*

WRITTEN & ILLUSTRATED BY

TASH TURGOOSE

Four hundred and ninety seven days.
That's how long she'd been down there.

One year, four months and thirteen days of jail cell
sunrises, and lost full moons.

Kept sane only by the creak of her ceiling as he tiptoed
over it to his bedside, and the letters posted through the
floorboards, saying all of the things they weren't allowed
to say out loud.

Then, on the weekends, he would post the pages of books,
one by one. A serial story, delivered from the sky.

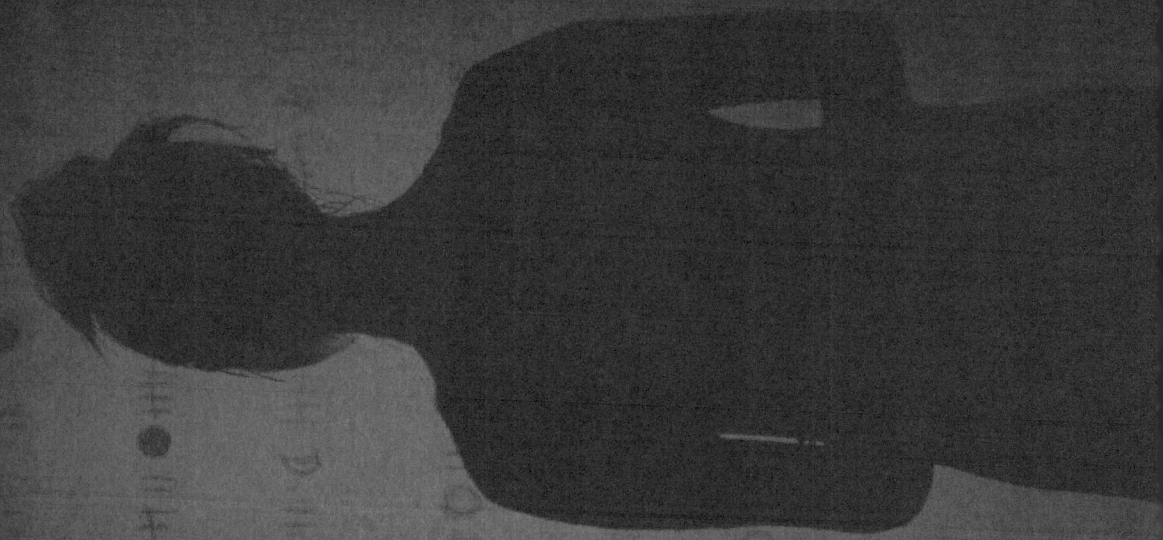

Sometimes, on the very best days, he would leave his curtains open, and sunrise would flood the room and leak through the floor boards, and fill her soul with sunshine.

On those days, she felt a little more human.

A little less buried in the silence.

Her last day of freedom had been a blur.

They arrived at day break, leaving only moments
for a final embrace before she was forced into her cell.

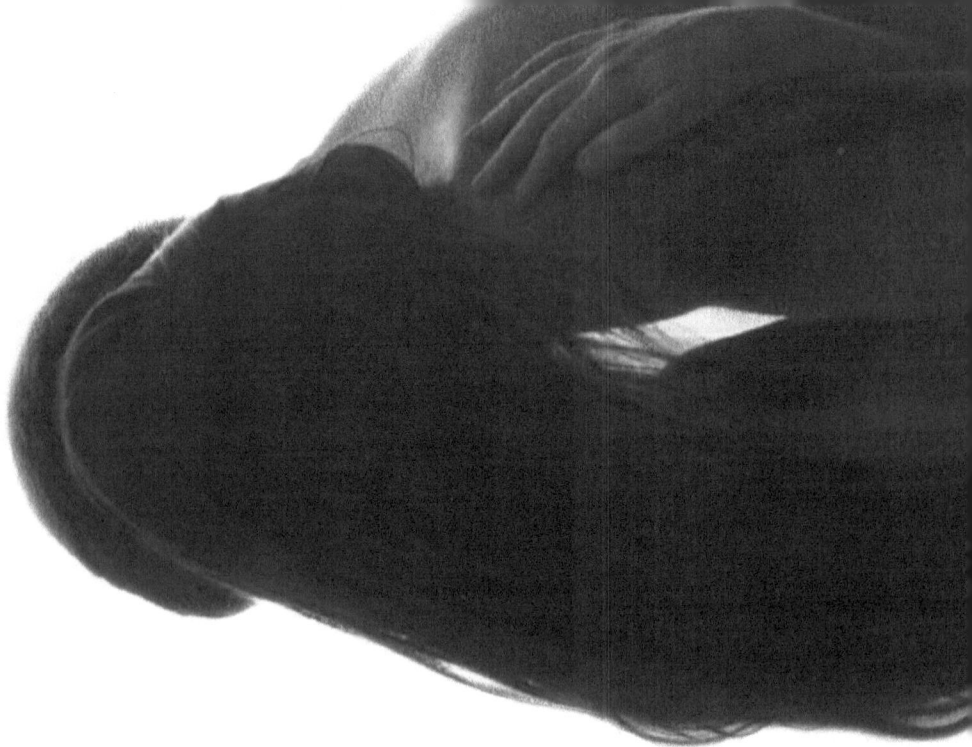

Nail, by nail,
she was hidden away

from a place she no longer belonged.

It was hard not to focus on the outside world.

Everything she was escaping.
Everything she was missing.

So, she escaped into other worlds, as she waited
for her own to welcome her home.

Hiding patiently, as she waited for it all to end.

Every day they posted letters, photos, drawings.
One time, even a rose.

Though, that didn't quite fit.

But nothing could replace how it felt to be alive,
outside, in the stolen sunshine,
in amongst the rainfall, the snow, the sea.

'The stars.

That's what I miss most,' she whispered. She could see his silhouette lying above her, and she traced it with her fingers.

'I used to count them when I couldn't sleep. But now, I can never sleep. There's no stars, or moon. I wish the galaxies could drip through the floorboards, like the sun. But instead, there's just darkness. Always, always darkness.'

She heard a shuffle, and the shadow lifted, then drifted away.

He returned a few minutes later, and slumped down onto the floor – then, a noise she didn't know. Scraping, twisting, grinding into the wood, before a metal skewer dipped through the floorboards. Then the noise started again.

Her laugh bounced through the floor.

'What do you think you're doing, poking holes into my sky?'

'Close your eyes,' he said. 'I'll tell you when to open.'

'You can open them now.'

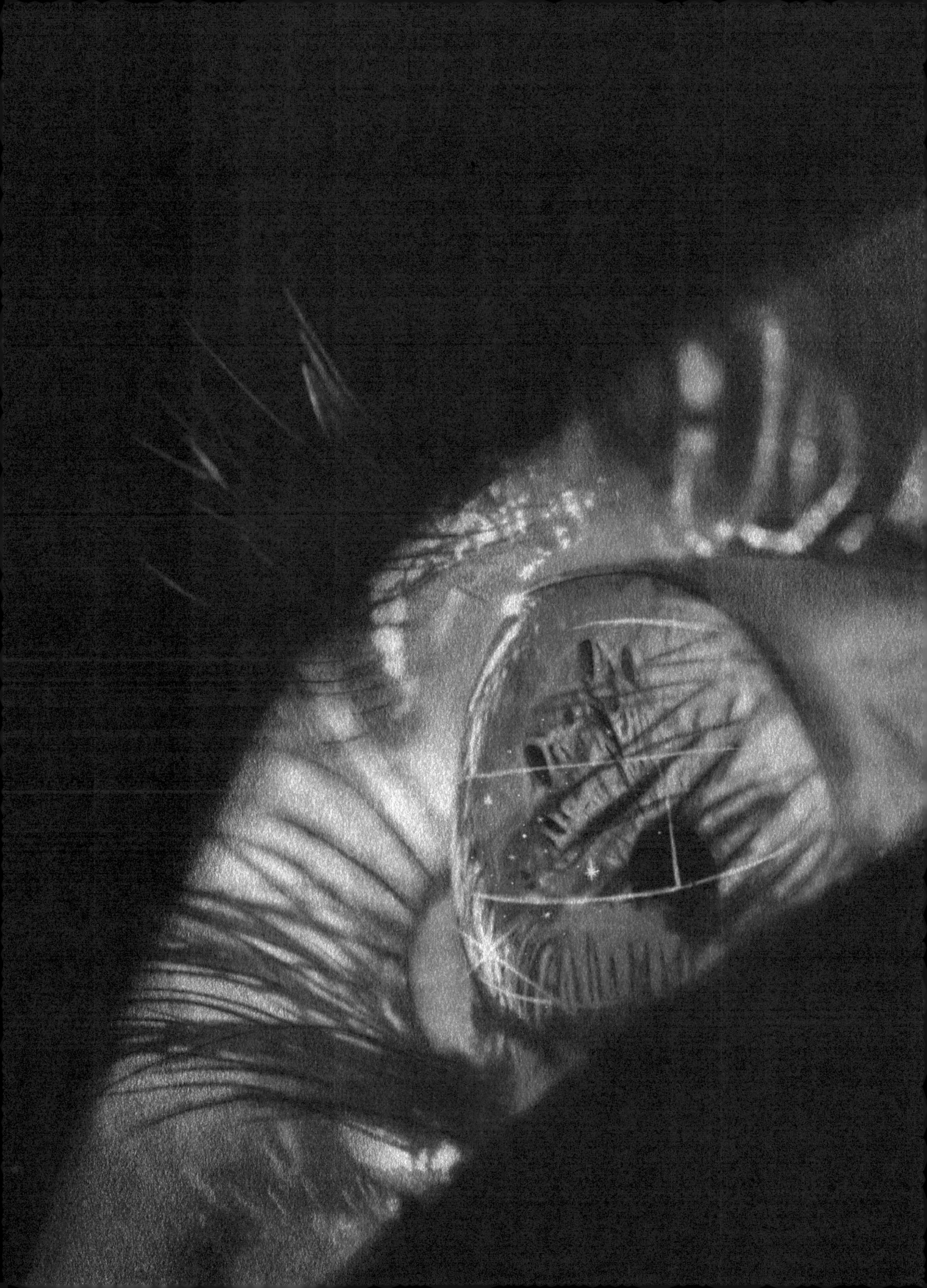

'Stars!' she whispered. 'My own makeshift galaxy!'

'Now you have to count them all. I'll expect an answer by tomorrow.'

She smiled, but her heart dropped. She longed to tear up the floorboards and wrap herself in his arms.

It would be worth the risk.

Almost.

It was a bizarre feeling, being trapped, but not trapped. Forced to stay, but technically free to leave whenever she pleased. Oh, if she could only leave her cell for just one moment.

But, if she were seen...

She'd stay down there for a lifetime, than risk being seen.

She pressed her face to her ceiling as he lay down upon it.

'One day,' he whispered, 'all of this will be over, and we'll watch the stars together every night.'

'Promise?'

'Promise.'

'How is it out there? Will it be better soon?'

'I can only hope.'

'I heard they're burning all the books.'

'They're trying.'

'Did you save any?'

'Of course. For you.'

'You stopped posting me the newspaper.'

'I know.'

The silence screamed with stories left untold.

'Sometimes, I wish I was in there with you.'

'I'm willing to share.'

He laughed a tiny, hollow laugh. His sadness seeped from every note.

'I'll see you when I fall asleep,' he whispered, and his weight grew heavier on the floor above.

The next night, there was a commotion on the floor above.

A storm ripped through her sky.

First, the rolling thunder of footsteps, then flashes of lightning as someone strutted back and forth through the moonlight.

No greeting.

Was it him?

Was it definitely him?

Had somebody found out about her?

Did he turn her in?

Where would they take her?

Was she going to die?

Was he going to die?

Would they cut her hair?

Would they stamp her flesh?

Would they just shoot her?

Should she run?

Where would she run?

Will she ever see the stars again?

Why was this happening?

Why?

The man dropped to his knees above her, and suddenly – the sound of metal on wood. They had found her. She knew it. This was it.

The jagged breaths fell into a mass of sobs. His sobs.

Him.

'I can't do this anymore,' he whispered, splayed across the floorboards. 'Can't do what?' She panicked, her brain flooded with visions of being thrust out into the open, forced to live a ticking time bomb life. 'All of this. Everything. You wouldn't believe what has become of this world. It's – ' His inhale was broken. 'I need to see you.'

The metal scraping began again.

'What are you doing?' 'I need to see you.' 'You can't. Someone will hear.' 'I can.'

With every protest, the floorboard became a little looser, until eventually, a waterfall of moonlight cascaded onto her skin.

She closed her eyes and drank in the silver rays, and the tiny stream of fresh, new air. He watched her, enchanted. The moonlight greeted her like an old friend, playing in her chocolate locks and lighting up her eyes.

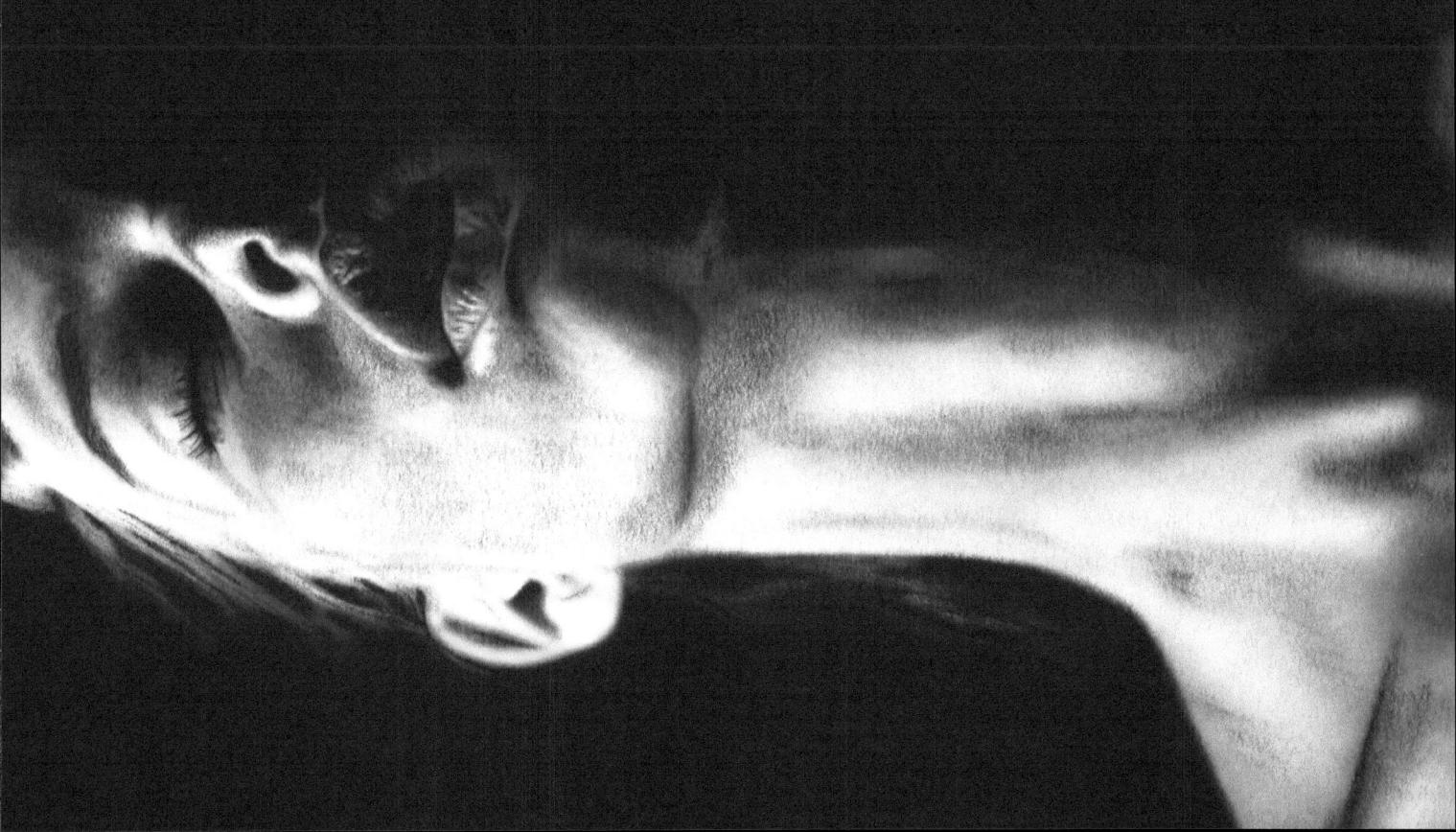

It was only supposed to be for a moment.
A single, fleeting moment of perfection.

9 781925 652154